Original title:
Sunlight Stories

Copyright © 2025 Creative Arts Management OÜ
All rights reserved.

Author: Elias Montgomery
ISBN HARDBACK: 978-1-80581-909-7
ISBN PAPERBACK: 978-1-80581-436-8
ISBN EBOOK: 978-1-80581-909-7

Chapters of Cheer

A squirrel in shades, taking a ride,
On a skateboard, oh what a slide!
With acorns in tow, he zooms about,
Cheering the birds with a noisy shout.

A dance contest starts near the big tree,
With rabbits in tutus, quite the sight to see!
They twirl and they flip, oh what a show,
The butterfly judges award them a trophy, though!

Radiating Through the Clouds

A cloud in a wig, such a funny disguise,
Puffs up with laughter, oh, how it tries!
It tickles the sun, sparks a chuckle or two,
While raindrops giggle, as if on queue.

Lightning bugs gather for a dance at night,
With glow sticks in hand, they feel just right.
Under the moon, they shine so bright,
Drawing stars in the air, what a lively sight!

Nature's Warmest Tales

The flowers bloom with cheeks so red,
They gossip about the bugs in bed!
Bees buzz the news with a pollen parade,
While the ants debate who gets the shade.

A turtle in shades plays on the grass,
Basking in sun, with a slow-motion class.
He teaches the rabbits to be chill and cool,
While the frogs all croak, 'This is quite the school!'

Portraits in the Horizon

The horizon paints with colors so wild,
A canvas of laughter, like nature's own child.
Clouds dressed in pink, giggle and sway,
While frogs dive in puddles just to play.

A rainbow appears, wears a silly hat,
Joking with the hills, 'I'm the colorful brat!'
Together they laugh as the sun says goodbye,
Painting the sky with a wink and a sigh.

Daybreak's Gentle Caress

The rooster crows a cheerful tune,
Bouncing rays beat the afternoon.
Cats chase shadows, oh what a sight,
Dancing around till they take flight.

Pancakes flip with a buttery glide,
Kids laugh loud, nowhere to hide.
Syrup spills like morning cheer,
Sticky fingers, smiles so sheer.

Bicycles wobble down the lane,
Dodging puddles from last night's rain.
A squirrel steals a sandwich with flair,
No crumbs left, just a happy stare.

Laughter echoes through the park,
As kids build castles that miss the mark.
Sand in toes and sunscreen smeared,
A day of fun that never feared.

Light's Embrace

A glow seeps through the window frame,
Like a bear warming in the flame.
Coffee brews with a whirring spin,
Awakening dreams where giggles begin.

Meanwhile, socks mismatch in a race,
As breakfast gets tossed in a wild chase.
Marmalade spreads like youthful glee,
Only the dog knows where it's to be.

Chirping birds gossip about the day,
While butterflies learn how to play.
A dance of shadows on the grass,
Making silly shapes that come and pass.

In the evening, twilight rolls in,
Candles flicker, and the banter spins.
Stories of clumsiness, laughter anew,
Bright moments shared by the merry crew.

Flickers of Optimism

A light bulb glows with a crackly laugh,
As bedtime tales take the oddest path.
Monkeys made of marshmallows soar,
While bedcovers hide ginormous snore.

Rainbow socks that never match,
Ready to cause a hilarious scratch.
Chasing dreams in unique style,
With giggles and shouts to last a while.

The sun peeks through the curtains wide,
Where sleepy heads can hardly bide.
With extra jumps and boundless play,
An optimistic start to a brand new day.

Even the fish are flipping mad,
Elaborate tales that make us glad.
With flickers of dreams in every heart,
Life's funny stories are a work of art.

Journey Through the Sunshine

On a road where shadows dance and twirl,
A hat flies off with a giggling whirl.
Ice cream cones melt into a splash,
Sticky faces with a joyous bash.

Sunflowers bobbing in a cheerful line,
Waving hello like they're sipping wine.
A dog fetches dreams without a care,
While children play tag with ruffled hair.

Picnic baskets burst with colorful treats,
Daring ants to pursue their feats.
Lemonade spills with a giggly splatter,
As laughter floats on the warm breeze's chatter.

As day fades out in a golden glow,
Fireflies dance, putting on a show.
With stars as friends, and dreams so bright,
The journey unfolds under the night.

Hues of Happiness

A plump cat slips on a ray,
Chasing shadows, in a playful ballet.
The dog laughs, wags with glee,
As the sun mocks their spree.

Lemonade spills, a sticky affair,
Ants parade in a sunlit square.
Friends gather, faces aglow,
In laughter, their worries bestow.

Jumping jacks on the green,
With each flip, the world feels keen.
Twirling, dancing, footloose and free,
Under the warmth of a giggling spree.

Chasing the breeze, kites in the sky,
A silly goose wanders by.
With every twist, the fun ignites,
As the sun spills joy, in delightful heights.

Epiphanies at High Noon

A squirrel dons sunglasses, so cool,
Pondering life like a wise ol' fool.
Chirping birds crack jokes in the trees,
As shadows dance with a teasing breeze.

The baker slips, flour takes flight,
His loaves all giggle, what a sight!
Pastries puff with a playful smirk,
In the oven, they plot their quirk.

A picnic blanket, a spilt snack,
Seagulls swoop, then dive with a clack.
Everyone laughs, it's all in good fun,
In this wacky high noon, under the sun.

Tickling toes in dusty parks,
Where laughter lands like tiny sparks.
The day beams bright, no hint of a frown,
As joy unfolds in this lively town.

The Lighted Path

Walking on sunshine, shoes made of glee,
A frog croaks puns, as funny as can be.
With each hop, he claims the way,
Making feet tap in a merry display.

The tallest trees wear crowns of laughter,
Rays of humor, there's no disaster.
A squirrel juggles acorns with flair,
While starlings chirp, filling the air.

Sidewalks bounce and giggle with pride,
As children skip, with joy as their guide.
A parade of chuckles fills the bright day,
In this vibrant realm, worries drift away.

Bananas peel back, revealing their grin,
Cheeky humor, where giggles begin.
Each step crackles with joy, oh so light,
On this path where laughter burns bright.

Glows of an Endless Afternoon

A puppy rolls in the sunbeam's glow,
Chasing his tail, proudly off he goes.
The ice cream drips, a colorful slide,
As laughter erupts like a joyous tide.

Hopscotch squares made of painted cheer,
As clouds play hide and seek, drawing near.
A silly dance-off breaks in the park,
With dandelions joining in—what a lark!

Grandma spins tales, her eyes full of spark,
Of mischievous fairies who laugh in the dark.
While the daisies nod, sensing the vibe,
Creating joy, they could hardly describe.

Bubbles float, catching the gleam,
Every pop echoes a childhood dream.
In this radiant haze, time tickles away,
In an endless afternoon, joy comes to stay.

Glistening Moments

A squirrel in shades, quite a sight,
Dances around in the bright light.
Dodging the rays like it's a game,
Whispers of laughter, never the same.

A puddle reflects a bird's flight,
With every splash, it springs with delight.
The world seems to giggle, how absurd,
Nature's soap opera, not quite unheard.

Caught in Time

A butterfly lands on a hat, oh dear,
The owner looks up, there's nothing to fear.
In a moment of bliss, they share a grin,
While the butterfly poses, ready to win.

A clock ticks loudly, time's up, they say,
But the butterfly lingers, just wants to play.
Caught in a dance with shadows and light,
Seconds turn into laughs, breezy delight.

The Warmth Beneath the Canopy

Under the leaves, a picnic is laid,
Ants start to join, thinking they've paid.
With sandwiches flying, a jelly jar too,
Nature's buffet, a feast for the crew.

A breeze whispers secrets, oh so bold,
While laughter erupts, stories unfold.
The trees shake their branches, a cheerleader's stance,
As crumbs fly like confetti, in a wild dance.

Chronicles of Daybreak's Glow

The rooster crows as shadows retreat,
While sleepy-eyed folks shuffle on their feet.
Coffee spills over, oh what a mess,
Turning morning chaos into laughter's best.

A dog steals a sock, it's quite the sight,
While kids chase giggles till the day turns bright.
The chronicles echo through laughter's embrace,
Morning shenanigans, a joyful race.

Honeyed Light Through the Leaves

Bees buzz around in a field of gold,
Sharing secrets and stories, bold and untold.
A flower takes a selfie, pollen on its face,
While all of nature joins in the chase.

A chase between shadows and playful gleams,
As laughter erupts like tiny sunbeams.
Every petal whispers, "Come and stay,"
In this honeyed light, we all want to play.

Echoes of Laughter Beneath Bright Skies

Chasing shadows in the park,
We trip on roots, oh what a lark!
With giggles shared, we tumble down,
Laughter flies, we wear a crown.

The dog steals fries from picnic plates,
While kids make faces, seal their fates.
A squirrel joins, it's quite the show,
As we forget all cares, let go.

Jokes bounce high, like kites in air,
We paint the world without a care.
Impromptu plays, we act so bold,
Each tale a gem, pure gold retold.

Beneath blue skies, memories bloom,
In every laugh, there's room to zoom.
The best stories start with a grin,
Echoes of joy, let the fun begin!

Where Rays and Dreams Intertwine

In a world where wishes fly,
We dance like fireflies, oh so spry.
With hats askew and shoes untied,
We leap through puddles, marks of pride.

Between the beams of golden light,
We spin our tales with sheer delight.
A robot dance or funny face,
Each silly slip finds its own place.

The laughter wraps around us tight,
As shadows grow, still hearts feel bright.
We craft our dreams with giggles spun,
A chase through rays, oh what a run!

In whimsical worlds where we retreat,
With every flick, we find the beat.
In these moments, gleefully we twine,
Creating joy, a spark divine!

Illuminated Pathways of Memory

Down the lane where echoes play,
We reminisce our funny fray.
With roadmaps drawn in crayon hues,
We chase the thrills, with laughs to muse.

Each step we take is filled with cheer,
As friends become the stories dear.
The wild goose chase around the tree,
Turns into tales of pure comedy.

Clowns in cars and hats too tall,
We fumble through the funniest fall.
With giggles shared on summer's breeze,
These moments cling, as memories seize.

In twilight's glow, we share a grin,
Recalling where our fun has been.
With every stitch of laughter sewn,
Illuminated tales are forever grown!

The Magic of Glowing Nostalgia

A wink, a nudge, the playful tease,
We paddle boats with wobbling knees.
Each gentle nudge a splash of fun,
As giggling echoes, we become one.

With glimmering eyes and hearts so light,
We chase the fireflies late at night.
Our fingertips touch the stars above,
Crafting memories wrapped in love.

Those silly hats we wore askew,
Bring back the antics of me and you.
As laughter twinkles through the air,
Magic glows in every shared stare.

We gather 'round the old oak tree,
Swapping tales in jubilee.
With every chuckle, we reacquire,
The golden glow of sweet desire!

Tales Written in Sunshine

A squirrel with shades, what a sight!
Dancing on branches, pure delight.
Chasing his tail, he slips and trips,
Leaves fall like laughter from his hips.

The flowers gossip, giggling away,
Telling the bees, 'What a funny day!'
They wear their colors, bright and bold,
Winking at the sun, secrets untold.

A cloud drifts by, looking quite shy,
While birds sing tunes, soaring high.
The grass tickles toes, a gentle tease,
Every moment here, a giggling breeze.

Laughter erupts, echoes of cheer,
Sharing their joy, day after year.
In this big playground, light plays around,
Every silly story in sunshine is found.

Threads of Daylight

A ladybug wears a polka-dotted hat,
Sipping on nectar, oh, how quaint is that!
She slides down a petal, a slippery ride,
With a giggle she lands, she's filled with pride.

The ants throw a party, marching in line,
Carrying crumbs and dancing divine.
They twirl and they twist, a parade on the ground,
With each tiny step, they jump all around.

The sun throws confetti, it sparkles and glows,
While a rabbit in socks hops high on his toes.
He tells all his buddies, 'Join in the fun!'
As shadows are cast, the day's just begun.

Chasing the giggles that float through the air,
Even the flowers can't help but share.
So gather your stories, let's laugh till we glow,
In this land of daylight, where funny things flow.

The Sun's Embrace

A cat in pajamas, lounging all day,
Rolling in sunlight, what a lazy ballet.
With a flick of her tail, she teases the air,
While the sun gives a wink, 'Come join if you dare!'

The children are running, all laughter and play,
Chasing shadow monsters that dance in the rays.
They trip over giggles, they leap and they slide,
With every bright moment, their joy cannot hide.

A dog picks a flower, oh what a delight,
Sniffing and snorting, he stumbles in flight.
With petals on his nose, he gives us a grin,
A portrait of happiness where joy begins.

In this golden garden, stories unfold,
Filled with mishaps, both funny and bold.
A playground of laughter, where sunshine is found,
Crafting sweet moments in warmth all around.

Festivals of Light

A dance of reflections, bright and absurd,
Fireflies jive while the crickets confer.
The owls are the DJs, spinning their tunes,
As stars join the party, twinkling with swoons.

A raccoon dons goggles and dives with a splash,
Stealing the scene in a wild moonlit dash.
With a belly full of berries, he laughs at the night,
In the festival of light, everything's bright.

Glowworms glow softly, lighting the way,
While frogs sing a chorus, making their play.
And the moon plays a game of hide and seek,
With bursts of surprise, it keeps us all weak.

So join in the revelry, dance if you may,
In this magical carnival where giggles don't stay.
Each moment a jewel, shining and free,
Crafting the tales of this wild jubilee.

Glimmers of Yesterday

In the fridge a light bulb glows,
Chasing cheese that almost froze.
Leftovers dance a funny jig,
While I munch on a rubber pig.

Socks with holes start to discuss,
Why they can't find their way to us.
Cupcakes frolic atop the shelf,
I swear they're plotting, not by oneself.

The cat dreams of a shiny fish,
While I ponder a spinning dish.
Laughter bursts in every nook,
Filling the pages of my book.

In the garden, weeds wear hats,
Hoping to join the acrobats.
Sunbeams giggle, playing hide,
As prankster shadows twist and slide.

The Horizon's Whisper

Balloons are bouncing, laughing high,
While ice cream spills make seagulls fly.
The sun pokes fun, a playful tease,
As flip-flops squeak and dance with ease.

A hat flew off, it's now a kite,
Chasing the breeze, took off in flight.
Children giggle, catch it quick,
While I just trip on a stick.

Jellybeans thrown in the air,
Land on noses, it's quite a scare.
Watermelons roll in glee,
Like they're plotting a bakery spree.

Frogs jump in for a silly swim,
While I can't help but do a whim.
Joy unravels under the sun,
In this circus of silly fun.

Daylight Diaries

Today my socks changed their hues,
They claim they danced with the morning dew.
Coffee's winking with a grin,
As I spill sugar, oh where to begin?

Pigeons gossip on the wire,
While I admire their feathery choir.
A dog in shades struts down the lane,
With swagger, he's the king of the plain.

Butterflies play hopscotch on flowers,
While the daisies cheer in bright towers.
Sunbeams tickle the garden fence,
A collective cheer, it's all quite tense.

Laughter echoes, oh what a sound,
As we stumble on candy wrappers found.
Juggling stories as we walk together,
Making memories as light as a feather.

Dazzling Pathways of Time

The clock is melting, can you see?
Time's gone wild, just like me.
Marshmallows bounce in a parade,
While I chase after my own shade.

Umbrellas up for the sunlight's show,
As ants march by, row by row.
Lemonade dreams bubble and swirl,
Where thoughts do cartwheels, twirl and whirl.

Glittering pathways lead the way,
With disco balls that gleefully sway.
Each grain of sand tells a tale,
Of silly rabbits who ride a snail.

Giggles echo through the air,
As clouds wear socks, but do you care?
Days rush by, but we don't mind,
In a mosaic of joy, we're intertwined.

Illuminated Journeys

We tripped on shadows, kicked some dust,
And rode our bikes without a fuss.
With every giggle, the sun got bright,
Chasing our dreams till the fall of night.

A dog chased us with awful glee,
Thinking we were some kind of tree.
We fell and rolled in fits of laughter,
Making memories, oh, what a disaster!

The ice cream melted, dripped like paint,
Swirled on our shirts, we looked quite quaint.
Oh, the sticky joy and wild-eyed thrill,
Every moment was pure, nothing still.

And when the sun finally dipped low,
We danced in the twilight, hearts aglow.
With silly stories and laughter, we spun,
Who knew growing up could be so much fun?

Fragments of Golden Time

We found a treasure, an old flip-flop,
Started a race, now we can't stop!
With toes all tan and laughter out loud,
We pranced like clowns, oh so proud!

A kite got stuck in a nearby tree,
We giggled as squirrels danced with glee.
The string unraveled as we took flight,
Chasing our dreams, what a silly sight!

A sandwich flew off during our feast,
A seagull swooped in like a hungry beast.
We laughed so hard we rolled on the sand,
How did lunch become a comedy band?

As the day waned to dusk's embrace,
We basked in our folly, a joyful race.
With sunlight fading, we waved goodbye,
To fragments of fun that soared the sky.

Laughter Beneath the Stars

At night we gathered, the sky a show,
With blankets spread out, and drinks aglow.
A rabbit hopped by, wearing a hat,
He stole our popcorn, imagine that!

We told tall tales of monsters and moons,
Swapped ghostly grins, like silly buffoons.
Our laughter echoed through the dark trees,
Spilling over like honey from bees.

A shooting star zipped, then went boom!
We made a wish, then tripped on a broom.
With twinkling eyes and laughter so bright,
We danced 'round the campfire, a glorious sight!

As the night faded, dreams took their flight,
We whispered our secrets with pure delight.
Beneath a canopy sparkling and vast,
We held onto joy, forever to last.

Radiant Pathways

We set off laughing, with snacks in tow,
Down dusty trails where the wild things grow.
Chasing butterflies, we slipped and fell,
Unearthed a story we know so well.

A twig in my hair made me quite chic,
You teased my style with a goofy peek.
Oh, the drips of joy from a juice box splat,
Each drop a memory in this sunny chat.

We built a fort with sticks and leaves,
Where we could hide from imaginary thieves.
A squirrel paid rent in acorn fines,
We wrote our laws in stick-figure lines.

As the sun dipped low, we called it a day,
With a sparkle of giggles that wouldn't fade away.
On radiant pathways, what fun we unveiled,
In our wild little world, how we joyfully sailed!

Whispers Beneath a Blazing Sky

A flaming ball above our heads,
The dog barks, joyously, in spreads.
We drench ourselves in lemonade,
As ants join in the big parade.

My ice cream cone melts down my hand,
While kids in shorts run down the sand.
Old man Fred has slipped yet again,
His hat now sails—oh, what a den!

The birds are chirping, full of cheer,
While squirrels plot mischief quite near.
A picnic blanket, spread with care,
Ends up as a trampoline chair.

Laughter bounces against the breeze,
Those sneaky wasps, they think they're bees!
We dance around, our spirits high,
In summer's warmth, we laugh and sigh.

Daydreams in Bright Light

In gardens lush, we skip and hop,
With sun-kissed cheeks, we never stop.
A frisbee flies, it finds a tree,
The branch is proud—it's home, you see.

The lemonade stand: a grand charade,
With spilled cups and plans remade.
A shout of joy, a trip, a fall,
Our giggles echo, one and all.

The kite is stuck, oh what a mess,
We tug and pull, who would've guessed?
Our fingers sticky, faces bright,
We chase the sunset, chasing light.

But in the end, it's all just fun,
With salty fries and laughter spun.
The brightest day, we dance and play,
In daydreams bright, we lose our way.

Sun-Drenched Memories

A beach ball's bounce, a splashy delight,
We race the waves, oh what a sight!
But one big wave, it steals the sand,
A treasure lost, right from our hand.

The BBQ grips the smoky air,
Where dads debate, and kids just stare.
A dance-off starts on summer grass,
When Grandma shows up, none can surpass!

The scents of sunscreen fill the breeze,
As someone shouts, "Get off your knees!"
The sun's too bright, our eyes go wide,
As memories bubble like the tide.

With laughter echoed, hearts aglow,
We wrap our day in undertow.
In moments sweet, we twirl and play,
In sun-drenched hues, we drift away.

Echoes of a Brighter Past

In golden rays, the stories flow,
Of childhood dreams we used to know.
A treehouse made from old scrap wood,
Where we once plotted all that's good.

An ice cream truck rolls down the street,
The sound of jingles makes hearts leap.
We chase it down with giddy glee,
Ice cream fate, for all to see!

The summers melt like buttered toast,
We laughed so loud, we'd brag and boast.
A slip and slide of pure delight,
The neighborhood kids, together tight.

Now we share those tales with grins,
Of splashes, laughter, and silly spins.
In echoes soft, we hear the past,
As sunlight dances, shadows cast.

Warm Embraces of the Afternoon

In the park, a dog does chase,
A squirrel with a lively pace.
Dodging trees, they twist and turn,
Sharing laughs, oh how they yearn.

A picnic spread, a sandwich flies,
Landing near a pair of flies.
They feast upon the crumbs, so sly,
With grape juice splashed, oh my, oh my!

A child spills juice, a sticky mess,
While ants celebrate their soft success.
With giggles loud, they cheer the day,
As bubbles float and drift away.

In afternoon's gentle glow,
The world becomes a funny show.
Laughter echoes far and wide,
As joy and chaos coincide.

Sunlit Secrets

A cat with shades lounges so fine,
Demanding treats, sipping on wine.
With every sunbeam, he takes a nap,
Dreaming of fish and a sunlit lap.

Children giggle and race around,
In search of treasures, lost and found.
A hidden stash of candy, oh dear!
Turns into chaos, laughter and cheer.

A kite gets stuck in a big green tree,
While a raccoon watches with glee.
Strangers join, all in good fun,
Shouting and laughing, under the sun.

As dusk approaches, tales unfold,
Of mishaps shared and secrets told.
In the glow of warmth, a quirky sight,
Life's mischief sparkles; all feels right.

Dappled Narratives

Beneath a tree, they start to plot,
A treasure hunt on the very spot.
With maps that crinkle, and giggles bright,
They race till dusk, what a silly sight!

A squirrel becomes their clever guide,
As they trip and stumble, what a ride!
Chasing shadows, they leap and bound,
With laughter echoing all around.

A dog sneaks snacks from the picnic spread,
Leaving crumbs behind as he fled.
The chase is on, with barks and screams,
In dappled light, they dance like dreams.

As twilight falls, tales weave and blend,
Of funny mishaps and the joy they send.
Under the stars, they recount their quests,
With hearts so happy, they are truly blessed.

Chronicles Under the Sky

Gathered 'round, they share a laugh,
A tale of socks, a funny gaffe.
One sock gone, another stuck,
In a dog's mouth, oh what luck!

A kite that spun, then took a dive,
With giggles that made them feel alive.
As ice cream drips down little chins,
The laughter grows, that's where it begins.

The clouds float by, a cotton ball,
Imagination takes off, past the wall.
Unicorns prance, and fish can fly,
In stories told under the vast sky.

As night draws near, they bid goodbye,
With hearts aglow, beneath the sky.
Chronicles shared, laughter so bright,
They promise to meet, for more delight.

Radiant Echoes of Yesterday

In a garden where gnomes dance,
They giggle in the sun's bright glance.
Flowers wear hats, buds prance about,
As bees line up for a sweet route.

Old squirrels joke, their tails a swirl,
The breeze joins in, gives it a twirl.
A hammock hums a tune of cheer,
While shadows whisper, 'We are here!'

The cat in shades dreams of a mouse,
As ants march by, plotting their house.
Laughter echoes through the trees,
The world, it seems, has caught a breeze.

Yesterday's picnics, where cake was chased,
Left crumbs for rabbits, who never paced.
We toast to those who laugh and share,
As sunlight scribbles stories rare.

Glowing Moments

A bug on a leaf plays peek-a-boo,
With a spider who waves while making his dew.
They giggle and hop on a candy treat,
The world's a playground, oh so sweet!

Clouds drift by with cheeky grins,
While squirrels start naming the winds.
A sunflower tips his hat with pride,
'Come dance with me!' says Sunshine outside.

Kids chase shadows that flicker and fade,
While sunbeams laugh at the games they played.
In this merry mix of laughter and light,
Every moment shines, oh so bright!

The sun sets gently, yet still holds tight,
To youthful spirits that spark with delight.
What tales unfold when warmth sets free?
In glowing moments, we find the spree!

Painted Horizons

In a sky of crayon and cotton candy,
The sun throws colors, all sorts of dandy.
Birds wear shades of a vibrant hue,
While clouds chat secrets, just me and you.

Kites dance high, pretending to flee,
As ice cream melts on a warm, happy spree.
The grass tickles toes in a playful tease,
As laughter flutters in the playful breeze.

A dad with a grill sings silly tunes,
While children create imaginary moons.
Each sunset's brushstroke, gentle and bright,
Holds stories of joy that take flight.

Under painted horizons, we twirl and laugh,
With goofy grins and a silly staff.
The sky's a canvas, our dreams take flight,
In a world where everything feels just right.

Sweet Sagas of Summer

Bikes zoom 'round on the sun-kissed street,
With a dog in tow, life feels so sweet.
Lemonade laughter with ice-cold cheer,
Every sip whispers, 'Stay right here!'

The park is alive with jump-rope games,
As kids gather 'round to claim funny names.
The tickle of grass, an impish delight,
While shadows stretch out, embracing the light.

Fireflies twinkle in a dusk dance,
While crickets orchestra a summer romance.
The moon joins in for a cheeky flair,
As night wraps softly with a cuddly care.

Sweet sagas told 'round the crackling fire,
With marshmallows roasting, electric desire.
In each glowing moment, we bravely explore,
The funny side of life, who could ask for more?

Reflections in the Morning Dew

A drop of dew hangs on the grass,
Like a tiny crystal ball, oh, so brass.
It reflects my morning bedhead style,
I chuckle at my hair—it surely won't beguile.

A ladybug poses, quite full of cheer,
Waving like a celebrity, oh dear!
It zooms off, leaving behind a cold glare,
Guess being cuter means no time to spare.

The flowers gossip, petals all a-flutter,
'Look at that snail, he's such a butter!'
They giggle and wiggle in amusing delight,
Call me old-fashioned; I'll join in their flight.

As dawn wakes up, the world starts to play,
I wonder what mischief we'll find in the fray.
With each beam of light, laughter is stored,
Morning's bright antics—a true comic record!

The Play of Blossoms in the Daylight

Daisies hold hands, twirling in a cheer,
While tulips declare, 'We're the stars of the year!'
A butterfly quips, 'Nature's runway tonight,'
Stumbling on petals, oh what a sight!

The sun turns on colors; the daisies blush red,
While roses in scandal just shake their proud heads.
"I'm just too pretty, I can hardly take note,"
Said a pansy as it tried to strut and gloat.

With bees as the DJ, buzzing a tune,
The flowers dance wildly, lost in their swoon.
"Step left, step right, now back to the center!"
A gladiolus laughs, "Why do I feel so tender?"

In this garden disco, oh what a delight,
Blossoms are laughing from morning till night.
In petals and pollen, joy does not dim,
They bloom to the beat; their happiness swims!

A Symphony of Light

The sun plays the flute as it starts to rise,
While shadows take turns, making awkward sighs.
"Hey, is that a cloud or just a big fluff?"
As laughter erupts, they're never quite tough.

The grass tries to mimic the sun's bright refrain,
Waving its blades as if to entertain.
"Let's throw in some giggles, mix them with rays,"
The breeze hums a melody; oh, how it sways!

Little ants dance, a marching band's pride,
Even the pavement adds to the ride.
Together they bounce in a whimsical show,
This orchestra of light puts on quite the glow!

As twilight whispers, "The show must conclude,"
The sunlight bows down, its essence renewed.
In each spark and shimmer, joy fills the night,
Their vivid performances—a pure, gleeful sight!

Stories Carved in Shadows

Shadows stretch like silly balloons,
Dancing along to the afternoon tunes.
A cat takes a peek, bemused and quite sly,
"Oh, how I love these shadow puppets by!"

The trees gossip tales of their ancient queens,
While puddles reflect surrealistic scenes.
A fawn trips on thin air, creates a big splash,
Even the shadows can't help but dash!

Frisking around like jesters enchanting,
Each twist and turn makes daylight commanding.
A squirrel wearing shades just stole the show,
Yes, even the shadows have places to go!

In a world turned playful where giggles erupt,
Every shadow tells stories; they never corrupt.
Tales filled with whimsy on a stage, oh so bright,
Here in the limelight, all laughter takes flight!

Secrets of a Sun-Kissed Afternoon

A squirrel in a tiny hat,
Danced atop my garden mat.
He pirouetted on a stone,
While I chuckled all alone.

The flowers giggled, bright and bold,
Watching antics, tales unfold.
A bee buzzed in, a tiny drone,
Claiming this patch as its own.

The clouds, they winked, a fluffy crew,
Puffing themselves, as if on cue.
A twig, a stick, oh what a find,
Turning my thoughts quite unrefined.

And as the sun began to dip,
I spilled my juice, a little slip.
Laughter echoed, just me and me,
In this warm, absurdity.

Flickers of Hope in Morning Mist

The rooster crowed, with quite a flair,
Awoke the world, everywhere.
Yet in his haste, he knocked a shoe,
A cluck of laughter, oh what a view!

The morning dew, like tiny pearls,
Danced on petals, spun in swirls.
A snail slid by, moving real slow,
With a sign that read, 'Just taking it slow!'

Butterflies sadly missed their flights,
Chasing each other, but lost in sights.
With wings that fluttered, they'd collide,
Buzzing with giggles, oh what a ride!

And as day broke with a splash,
Pancakes flipped, in golden flash.
Together we chuckled, as dawn's first light,
Brought joy in mist, oh, what a sight!

Through the Veil of Daylight

A cat in sunglasses, cool as can be,
Stretched on the porch, sipping sweet tea.
With a flick of its tail, it surveyed the trees,
As if judging life's pace, with unfazed ease.

The shadows played hide and seek,
With ants that marched, all bold and sleek.
A ladder made of branches, oh what a sight,
All just to reach that last cookie bite!

Giggles erupted from a bright, green frog,
Pondering life from his perch on a log.
He sang a tune, quite offbeat, you see,
A serenade fit for a bumblebee!

As daylight danced in a glorious show,
We chuckled together, a warm-hearted glow.
From silly to sweet, every moment bright,
In that happy veil of the golden light.

Light's Gentle Caress on Still Waters

A fish in a bowler hat, quite dapper,
Swam in circles, like a smart rapper.
He'd twirl and splash, with a wink and grin,
As the tadpoles laughed at the show he'd spin.

The trees encircled, a silent cheer,
Glistening leaves laughed, "Let's gather near!"
A dragonfly buzzed, with a comic glide,
It crashed in the pond, oh how it cried!

The ripples danced like a jigging crew,
Catching whispers of jokes anew.
A duck quacked loudly, with quite the flair,
Saying "All aboard for the funnest scare!"

As light cascaded on this silly scene,
The laughter blossomed, pure and serene.
Waves of joy seemed to knit us tight,
In this playful space, everything felt right.

Glimmers of Joy in the Meadow

In the meadow where daisies bloom,
A rabbit jumps, who could assume?
With floppy ears and a comic hop,
He dodges bees, he just can't stop!

Beneath the trees, a squirrel sneaks,
With acorns piled, he's got techniques.
He glances left, he glances right,
In his little world, it's quite a sight!

The grass whispers jokes to the breeze,
Tickling toes, oh, such a tease!
A butterfly twirls, and then takes flight,
Chasing shadows, what a delight!

With giggles from streams that trickle near,
Nature beams, it's perfectly clear,
In this rich hue of greens and gold,
Life's a jest, forever bold!

The Language of Warmth and Light

A sunbeam chats with a playful cloud,
Waving hello, feeling quite proud.
The leaves all giggle, they sway in cheer,
As shadows dance, bringing good cheer!

A ladybug lands on a sunlit rock,
Declares it's time to have a talk.
With her tiny voice, she shares her plan,
To throw a party for every fan!

A sudden gust sends petals whirling,
As joyous laughter sets hearts twirling.
The flowers nod, they all agree,
It's the best kind of jubilee!

With joy that hums in every ray,
The light-hearted whispers lead the way.
It's in the warmth of a sunny gleam,
That nature holds a lively dream!

Shadows Play in Radiant Harmony

A shadow leaps from behind a tree,
Hiding and seeking, oh so free!
It stretches wide, it dances near,
Chasing giggles, spreading cheer!

The sun winks down on this playful scene,
As ants in a line march, so routine.
A butterfly flits by, hopping along,
Creating a chorus of nature's song!

A breeze swoops in, causing a stir,
Throwing whispers where laughter spur.
Each little critter joins in the fun,
Playing tag until day is done!

Under the sky, oh, what a sight,
Shadows laugh with delight, so bright.
In the dance of light and shade so spry,
Even the sun beams down to sigh!

Sunbeams Paint the Sky

With a dash of yellow and a splash of blue,
Sunbeams swirl, creating a view!
They tickle the clouds, they brush the trees,
While birds join in with goofy tweets!

A rainbow drops by, wearing a grin,
Chasing raindrops, oh let the fun begin!
It paints the hopes, it sparkles bright,
A canvas of joy in broad daylight!

Kites flutter up, like they've lost their mind,
Swinging and swooping, what a find!
Each tug and pull brings laughter anew,
As the sky's a theater of vibrant hue!

The sun sets low, with an orange cheer,
It whispers stories for all to hear.
With warmth and giggles, it bids goodnight,
Dreaming of dances till the dawn's light!

Golden Glimmer of Hope

A squirrel donned shades with flair,
He danced on branches, without a care.
His acorn stash? It vanished fast,
He claims it's magic, a spell he cast.

The sun peeked in, with a wink so bold,
The grass grew tall, but alas, too old.
A frolicsome rabbit, with quite a hop,
Stole all the carrots before they could crop.

A picnic planned, with treats galore,
But ants arrived, and then came more.
They nibbled sandwiches, snuck in some pie,
Left only crumbs to my dismay and sigh.

Yet laughter erupted, joy in the air,
As clouds puffed up, looking like bears.
A sunny day, with giggles spread wide,
What stories unfold when we let fun abide!

Tales in the Light

A cat in a hat, oh what a sight,
Chasing sunbeams with all its might.
It tripped on its tail, rolled over too,
But continued its quest for the light so true.

Two dogs played tag, under rays of gold,
One found a stick, which turned into bold.
The wagging tails told tales so bright,
As shadows danced in the fading light.

A child on a swing, soaring up high,
Tickled by sunbeams that danced through the sky.
They giggled at clouds, soft as a dream,
While bees buzzed around with a whimsical theme.

In laughter we gather, no time to fret,
For in shining moments, joy won't forget.
A day filled with tales where smiles ignite,
We weave all our stories in the beautiful light.

Luminous Days Unfolding

A frog in a pond, with a crown on its head,
Recited some verses, and off went the spread.
The dragonflies laughed, splashing with glee,
As the pond turned into a circus marquee.

A snail in a race, said, "Hold on a sec!"
While onlookers cheered, what the heck?
With sun on its shell, it took a bold stance,
Winning the gold in a slowpoke dance!

A bird chirped jokes from atop a tall tree,
Tickling the leaves, with its melody.
A chorus of laughs joined in the song,
As fireflies flicked their lights all along.

Now evening descends, the glow still remains,
With tales of delight and whimsical gains.
In laughter, we wrap all our luminous dreams,
A day filled with fun, like flowing sunbeams.

Beams of Joy

A pancake flipped with a squeal in the air,
Land on the roof? No one would dare!
It plopped on a dog, who gave a loud bark,
Now breakfast is fun, all thanks to this lark.

With sunlight draping over the scene,
A kite flew high, quite the vibrant queen.
The wind took a turn, the string in a twist,
As it danced with the clouds, oh what a list!

A picnic spread wide, with fruit and cheese,
But seagulls on patrol brought us to our knees.
They swooped in like pirates, claiming their prize,
With raucous laughter, we laughed till we cried.

So cheers to the moments, bright and bizarre,
Where every mishap becomes a new star.
With beams of pure joy lighting the way,
We're weaving our tales, come dance and play!

The Enchanted Glow

In a garden so bright, with flowers in cheer,
A gnome lost his hat, and the bees drew near.
They buzzed all around, such a silly sight,
That gnome in his panic, took off in flight.

A squirrel then chuckled, with acorns to show,
He found the lost hat, and put on quite a show.
With laughter they danced, in a whimsical way,
Under beams of pure gold that brightened the day.

The rabbit joined in, with a wiggle and hop,
He twirled with delight, never planning to stop.
Each critter a player, in this grand charade,
While shadows and laughter together were made.

As dusk crept upon them, they twinkled like stars,
With stories of mischief, and all of their scars.
In the glow of the moon, they would chuckle and grin,
Revealing their secrets, the magic within.

Moments Bathed in Light

A cat with a hat stepped into the sun,
He pranced on the pavement, just having some fun.
His friends in the yard gathered round for a treat,
As they plotted mischief, on little cat feet.

The dog chased a butterfly, round and around,
While the parrot mimicked what it thought was a sound.
With each silly step, the laughter took flight,
Capturing moments so pure and so bright.

The flowers would gossip, their petals abloom,
Sharing tales of the mischief that whirled 'round the room.
"Oh look at that squirrel, he's stealing my shine!"
The daisies would whisper, as they stretched on the line.

And as golden rays dipped a bit low in the sky,
They'd bask in the warmth, letting giggles fly high.
For even in trouble, they'd always find cheer,
Transforming each moment to laughter sincere.

Meys of Dawn

At dawn there's a rooster, who thinks he's a king,
He crows at the sun, like it's his favorite thing.
With a clap of his wings, he struts oh so proud,
Dancing 'round shadows, he sings to the crowd.

The bunnies awake, with a hop and a squeak,
They're planning a party, with carrots to sneak.
The whole meadow chuckles as they make their rounds,
Dancing through dew drops, with giggles and sounds.

A fox on the hill, with a sly little grin,
Snuck in for a snack, hoping no one would win.
But the owls all winked, with a twinkle in eyes,
He dashed off in fright, oh, what a surprise!

In the pinkness of morn, the laughter took flight,
With a wink from the sun, all was merry and bright.
Each creature a jester, in nature's grand play,
Embracing the humor that blossomed each day.

Lively Sketches of the Sky

A cloud shaped like pizza, floated by with a grin,
While a rainbow teased thunder, who'd never let in.
The sun painted hues, on a canvas so vast,
With joy in the air, their antics amassed.

Kites soared like eagles, untamed in the breeze,
They whispered to dandelions, dancing with ease.
A kite caught a tree, and the branches said "Hey!"
What a ruckus they made, in their playful display.

A cheeky old crow played tricks on a snail,
It borrowed his shell for a whimsical tale.
Three squirrels rolled dice, on the back of a frog,
When the sun threw down warmth, creating a smog.

With laughter and whispers, the sky came alive,
In a world of pure mirth, where the silly can thrive.
Each sketch was a memory, a moment well-caught,
In this lively domain, where joy's never sought.

Season of Brightness

A squirrel in shades, dancing with glee,
He found a acorn, oh me, oh me!
While birds sing a tune, in a wobbly chat,
The wind whispers secrets, how about that?

With daisies chuckling in a field full of cheer,
A rabbit made coffee, with a flick of a ear.
The bees swung in rhythm, a comical sway,
Buzzing about life in their own happy way.

Old trees tell tales, with branches that wave,
While clowns of the forest, the creatures behave.
A fox on a unicycle, what a view!
As laughter erupts, the moments shine through.

So grab your sunshine and dance with delight,
In a world of weird wonders, oh what a sight!
For every bright giggle, and snicker so wide,
We paint with our laughter — let joy be our guide.

The Golden Tape

There's a roll of gold tape, stuck on a shelf,
That claims it's a genie, just wish for yourself!
But when I unroll, it just sticks to my hand,
It won't let me go, it has its own plan!

I wished for a bicycle, sleek as a dream,
But got a unicycle, bursting at the seam.
With a honk and a wobble, I rode down the lane,
And passed by a goat who laughed at my pain!

The tape then decided to take a quick spin,
Wrapped around the dog, oh where to begin?
He zoomed through the yard like a bright shooting star,
Chasing after squirrels, yeah that's who we are!

We laughed till we cried, in a glittery mess,
Golden dreams tangled, but who needs finesse?
In this goofy adventure, we all play our part,
Embracing the chaos, with a kid's merry heart.

Warmth Under the Canopy

Under the leaves, the shadows play fair,
A turtle tells jokes, in his cozy lair.
With painted-on smiles, the frogs join the fun,
Croaking their laughter, in the warm sun.

A bear with a hat, sipping sweet tea,
Sifting through stories, as happy as can be.
The bumblebees boogie with a twirl and a spin,
While ants tap dance — oh, let the party begin!

Mushrooms are mushrooms, but some play guitar,
Singing about summer and how sweet things are.
Then suddenly, boom! A rain cloud appears,
But the critters just chuckle, they've got no fears.

For even in showers, they splash and they prance,
Wading through puddles, each has a chance.
So come one, come all, to this whimsical fest,
Where warmth and pure laughter simply manifests.

Stories of Dappled Light

In dappled light, where the giggles abound,
A cat in a hat is the talk of the town.
He juggles and tumbles, with fish in his paws,
Oh, the crowd's in stitches, let's hear those applause!

A rabbit named Benny, with his big floppy ears,
Tells tales of adventures, and ticklish fears.
With flashlights and shadows, they laugh through the night,
Every story's a journey, from fright to delight!

The trees become actors, bowing with flair,
While critters in costumes dance without a care.
A fox in a vest, struts a delicate line,
"Oh, let's not forget," he says, "I'm divine!"

So gather the pals, the tales just don't cease,
In the dappled light glow, we find our peace.
With laughter our language, and joy as our guide,
This funny old world fills us up with pride.

Dancing with Dawn's Embrace

The rooster crows, a waking cheer,
As morning yawns, the world pulls near.
Pajamas sway in the gentle breeze,
While coffee spills—oh, such a tease!

The cat does somersaults on the bed,
Chasing sunlight where dreams once spread.
Bouncing like a ball, he leaps with zest,
Yet lands in toast—oh, what a jest!

Birds sing loudly in silly trills,
While dancing squirrels do backflips on hills.
Giggles escape as shadows play,
Around the trees, they twirl and sway.

With every beam, the day begins,
In a wild race, and nobody wins.
But laughter echoes above the ground,
In this joyful dance we have found.

Whispers of the Golden Hour

The clocks are ticking, but who can tell?
In a golden glow, we weave a spell.
The dog wears shades, looking quite cool,
While kids make up rules, acting a fool.

Lemonade stands with laughter abound,
Conversations echo, simple and profound.
A ladybug lands on a pint of fries,
And giggles erupt as a friend tries.

The sunset spills its colors wide,
As neighbors gather, all taking pride.
In oversized hats and bubbly drinks,
We share our tales and what each thinks.

As day grows dim, we toast to cheer,
To silly moments we hold so dear.
In whispers soft, our secrets glide,
As twilight dances, and dreams collide.

Radiance in the Quiet

In quiet corners where shadows lay,
A squirrel drops acorns in playful fray.
The sun peeks in with a wink of fun,
And tickles the grass as it starts to run.

A butterfly lands on a sleepy cat,
He sneezes wildly and then says, "What's that?"
The world bursts forth in a chuckling roar,
As children burst out of the nearby door.

Whispers of mischief float in the air,
As bubbles pop in a bubbly stare.
A dance party starts with make-believe,
Where everyone twirls and no one leaves.

Laughter rolls like a gentle stream,
While doodles of joy fill every dream.
And in this moment, all's perfectly right,
As tranquility mingles with sheer delight.

Tales from the Luminous Horizon

The horizon glows, a canvas bright,
With tales of antics that feel just right.
A gopher pops up with a grin so wide,
Surprise! Wait, where's all his pride?

Little feet scatter, to run and chase,
While laughter bubbles in a frenzied race.
Ice cream drips down a cheeky nose,
And everyone's giggling as chaos grows.

A kite flies high, stuck in a tree,
And pretend superheroes yell, "Let it be!"
With capes on back, they swoosh and glide,
As each little adventure starts to collide.

So here's to the tales that fill our days,
In luminous hues where joy stays ablaze.
With every chuckle, the world we explore,
In these silly moments, who could want more?

Memoirs of a Sunbeam

A beam once claimed a dancing chair,
That jumped around without a care.
It twirled and spun till all were dizzy,
To giggle at shadows, quite busy.

It poked at flowers with a grin,
To tickle petals and make them spin.
The roses laughed, 'Oh what a play!
This sunbeam's here to brighten the day!'

One day it tried to catch a cat,
But missed its tail and landed flat.
The cat just stared, then gave a yawn,
'You silly light, I'm out at dawn!'

Yet every evening as it retreats,
It finds new tales in cozy seats.
In every corner, laughs and glee,
The sunbeam tells its wild spree!

Heartbeat of the Day

A ticklish glow upon the grass,
Chased ants around, quite like a class.
The flowers waved in sheer delight,
'Oh look, here comes the day so bright!'

It giggled softly, leaped a bit,
And gave a worm a friendly hit.
'You should thank me for this shine,
Now wiggle free, it's lunch time fine!'

The clouds rolled by with smirks and sneers,
'Trying to steal our playful cheers!'
But the glow just laughed and danced away,
'I'm only here to warm the day!'

At dusk, it whispered jokes to stars,
About the antics of passing cars.
With every chuckle, hearts did sway,
A heartbeat traced in golden play!

Skylit Narratives

In the morning, with yawns and grins,
The sky wrote tales of silly sins.
Clouds in hats, a stormy consent,
Turned rain into a slide event!

Birds soared high, playing tag with light,
While shadows chased them in delight.
A rainbow winked, oh what a tease,
'There's magic here, if you please!'

The sun played tricks with hiding beams,
Peek-a-boo, bursting into dreams.
Each laugh unfurled like morning dew,
Sky stories shared, for me and you.

As dusk painted lines of peach and rose,
The tales kept coming, as night arose.
Each star took turns in this grand play,
In skylit narratives that won't sway!

Reflections in Gilded Hues

A puddle smiled and caught the light,
While ducks went quacking, such a sight!
They splashed and flapped in gleeful arcs,
With golden glimmers dancing sparks.

The trees above joined in the sway,
'We're the ones who laugh and play!'
With rustling leaves they told their fables,
Of games with moonbeams and round tables.

The sunbeams giggled at the show,
'The more we shine, the more we glow!'
So every sparkle on the ground,
Burst forth like laughter all around.

As twilight draped its cozy quilt,
The tales of light were softly spilt.
In reflections bright, the joy renews,
With gilded moments, oh what hues!

Twilight's Gentle Embrace

The moon stole the sun's golden grin,
As shadows danced, let the laughter begin.
A cat in a top hat, strutting down the street,
Claiming he's the king, oh what a treat!

A firefly flickered, not quite a star,
Said, 'I'm a taxi! Please hop in, ajar!'
Bumblebees giggled, buzzing in flight,
Dropping their pollen with pure delight!

The flowers joined in, they wiggled and swayed,
Spinning around in a bright, flowery parade.
In the twilight's embrace, all troubles take flight,
And laughter echoes until the dark night.

So here's to the twilight with its whimsical flair,
Where giggles are free and whirling is rare.
Let's frolic and tumble till dawn decides,
To chase away giggles and curtain our rides!

The Sun-Kissed Chronicle

In a land where suns wore silly hats,
Chickens played chess, oh what is that?
A squirrel on a bicycle zoomed by with glee,
Cackling with joy, just as happy as can be!

The clouds were cotton candy, fluffy and sweet,
While the rabbits had picnics that couldn't be beat.
And if you listened closely, you'd hear them roar,
A symphony of laughter from behind every door!

The sun waved its rays, a warm golden dance,
Making all critters throw caution askance.
They traded their woes for a tickle and cheer,
Creating a story that everyone could hear!

So gather 'round, friends, and don't be shy,
In this sun-kissed realm, let spirits fly.
With giggles and grins lighting up the day,
Every moment's a story, come join the play!

Illuminated Dreams

In a dream where cats wore mismatched socks,
A parrot recited the latest TikTok.
Stars twinkled brightly, tickling the sky,
While moons in pajamas sang lullabies!

A dog on a skateboard rolled right past me,
Chasing after comets, adventurous and free.
The trees told tall tales, with leaves a-shiver,
About rabbits who swam in the wide, blue river.

Every beam of light shared a joke of the night,
Telling secrets of crickets who played in delight.
With giggles like bubbles, they floated around,
In the land of dreams, where joy knows no bounds!

So let's dive in deep, where silliness reigns,
With every bright thought, the laughter remains.
In these illuminated dreams, let's make a toast,
To funny adventures we love the most!

Bright Footprints in Time

Footprints of laughter dance on the ground,
Where every step taken makes joy all around.
A frog in a tuxedo jumped high with flair,
Singing off-key, without a single care!

The sun threw a party, balloons in the air,
A parade of silly hats beyond compare.
With squirrels as DJs and hedgehogs in line,
The world twinkled back with laughter divine!

The clouds played hide and seek, drifting along,
While flowers swayed to a whimsical song.
They whispered sweet secrets, petals all aglow,
In this kaleidoscope where laughter can grow.

So mark your bright footprints, don't let them fade,
In the book of chuckles, where memories are made.
Let each step be funky, let each grin be wide,
In the journey called life, let laughter be your guide!

The Comet's Child: Where Warmth Meets Wonder

A comet's child laughs in the skies,
Chasing twinkling stars with gleeful cries.
He tickles the clouds till they bounce and sway,
Bringing giggles to the end of the day.

His friends the moons roll in silver hue,
They play hide and seek in the cosmic blue.
With playful beams, they paint the night,
Turning shadows to laughter, oh what a sight!

He steals the sun's warmth to share with the night,
Dancing in puddles of shimmering light.
A friend to the breeze, he sings with delight,
In this game of joy, everything feels right.

So join in the chase where the stardust flies,
With comet's child dreams, come color the skies.
Let's frolic through spaces, so wide and grand,
For warmth and wonder go hand in hand.

Harvesting Shadows in Radiant Fields.

In fields where shadows and laughter grow,
Silly scarecrows dance, putting on a show.
They tickle the corn as they sway to the beat,
Harvesting fun with each wobbly feet.

Bouncing beans jump, in the sun they delight,
Waving to clouds as they pirouette bright.
With roots digging deep, they chuckle and cheer,
While rabbits do cartwheels, with no hint of fear.

The sun plays peek-a-boo with the hills,
While butterflies whisper their tiny thrills.
The fruits grow bigger, oranges grin wide,
Sharing silly stories with nothing to hide.

We gather the laughter, we sow all the cheer,
In radiant fields, where the mirth draws near.
So harvest your shadows, let giggles resound,
For in this bright world, pure joy can be found.

Dancing Rays of Dawn

Dancing rays tiptoe on the waking ground,
Chasing off dreams with a soft, silly sound.
They wiggle through windows, tickling your toes,
As sleepyheads chuckle and rub their eyes close.

With breakfast in mind, they feel quite spry,
Slivers of sunshine that bounce as they fly.
Marmalade giggles spill over the toast,
While tea cups chuckle, they giggle the most.

The sleepy cat stretches, yawns wide, then leaps,
Chasing the light with its wild, woolly heaps.
The flowers burst open, in colors they flaunt,
Unfurling their petals with a whimsical taunt.

So rise up and dance with what dawn brings near,
Join in the laughter, let merriment steer.
For in the bright rays that twirl and they sway,
Lives the joy of today, come what may!

Whispered Warmth of Morning

In morning's embrace, a soft laugh is found,
As light spills like honey, wrapping the ground.
Whispered secrets tickle the sleepy air,
With frogs in their boots, who leap without care.

The toast pops up, it's doing a jig,
While coffee swirls round, feeling quite big.
The cat with a wink, gives a purring laugh,
As sunbeams join in for a cheerful gaff.

Birds gossip together in songs full of glee,
While squirrels are planning their grand jubilee.
They spin and they leap, all in lively trails,
While morning joins in with its tuneful tales.

Embrace this warm laughter that morning provides,
As the day unfolds with the light as your guide.
In this whispered warmth, let the fun begin,
For joy rides the breeze on the path we spin.

www.ingramcontent.com/pod-product-compliance
Lightning Source LLC
Chambersburg PA
CBHW070319120526
44590CB00017B/2746